HELP! i'm a small-group leader!

50 ways to lead teenagers into lively & purposeful DISCUSSIONS

Here's more *Help!* for youth leaders from Youth Specialties!

Help! I'm a Volunteer Youth Worker!
Doug Fields

Help! I'm a Sunday School Teacher!
Ray Johnston

Help! I'm a Junior High Youth Worker!
Mark Oestreicher

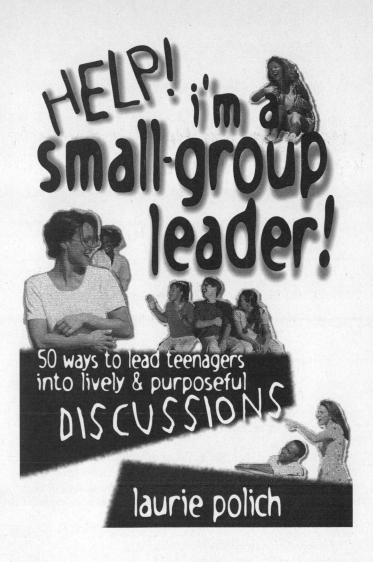

HELP! i'm a
small-group
leader!

50 ways to lead teenagers into lively & purposeful DISCUSSIONS

laurie polich

Youth Specialties

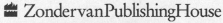
ZondervanPublishingHouse

Grand Rapids, Michigan
A Division of HarperCollinsPublishers

Help! I'm a Small-Group Leader!
50 ways to lead teenagers into lively & purposeful discussions

Copyright © 1998 by Youth Specialties, Inc.

Youth Specialties Books, 1224 Greenfield Dr., El Cajon, CA 92021, are published by Zondervan Publishing House, 5300 Patterson Ave. S.E., Grand Rapids, MI 49530.

Library of Congress Cataloging-in-Publication Data
Polich, Laurie.
    Help! I'm a small group leader : 50 ways to lead teenagers into lively & purposeful discussions / Laurie Polich
       p.   cm.
    "Youth Specialties."
    ISBN 0-310-22463-2
    1. Church group work with teenagers. I. Title.
BV4447.P56 1998
259'.23—dc21
                                    98-22388
                                      CIP

Unless otherwise indicated, all Scripture quotations are taken from the Holy Bible: *New International Version* (North American Edition). Copyright © 1973, 1978, 1984 by International Bible Society. Used by permission of Zondervan Publishing House.

Edited by Sheri Stanley and Tim McLaughlin
Cover and interior design by Curt Sell
Illustrations by Krieg Barrie

Printed in the United States of America

99 00 01 02 03 / / 10 9 8 7 6

CONTENTS

ACKNOWLEDGMENTS

Special thanks to—

- Stacy Sharpe, who has been my "small group" for two years, as we've helped each other see our circumstances through God's eyes.
- Mom and Buck, whose love and support has helped make life in Laguna feel like home.
- The Say Yes students and staff at Central City Community Church, who have taught me what it means to live as a dispenser of God's grace.
- Bill and Tracey Wertz, whose warmth and hospitality let me finish this book, feel at home in Bellingham, and spend lots of time in a hot tub.

INTRODUCTION

When I was 17, I had my first

small-group experience. It was February of my senior year. I had signed up to go to a Christian camp for the—ahem—very spiritual reason that my boyfriend was going, and I wanted to be with him (a common level of spirituality among high school students). But God wasn't constrained by my motives, and I came back from camp with a new relationship. Two weeks later, my boyfriend and I broke up, but God and I have been together ever since.

I became a Christian that weekend largely because of the patience and encouragement of my small-group leader. I can still see Joanne's face as I strongly asserted my spiritual views, misguided though they were. As I explained to her the Gospel According To Laurie Polich, she patiently listened to my ideas, trusting that the Holy Spirit would make the needed adjustments as time went on. Somehow she knew that all of us in the group needed a chance to process our thoughts and be heard. And thanks to Joanne's skilled leadership, our small group was a place where that could happen.

Since then I've been in all sorts of small groups, as a leader or a participant. Joanne's face has remained an image for me as I've tried to be the kind of small-group leader she was—the kind that students really need. I'm thankful for Joanne and so many others who, with gentleness, patience, and faithfulness, modeled for me what small-group ministry is all about. It's because of their work in my life that I've had the freedom and encouragement to fall so deeply in love with Jesus Christ.

Help! I'm a Small-Group Leader! is for people who want to impact students through the ministry of small groups. It's the most effective way I know to help kids grow in their faith. Perhaps it's because they experience firsthand—sometimes for the first time—the body of Christ. "From Christ the whole body, joined and held together by every supporting ligament, grows and builds itself up in love, as each part does its work," wrote Paul to the Ephesian church (4:16). As students join together in a supportive environment, they not only learn what it means to become a Christian, but how to be the Christian they've become. This is true discipleship.

There are all sorts of ways to effectively lead a small group, yet most of these ways are distilled from a few proven principles. This book equips you with these principles, while letting you keep the uniqueness of your own style. "There are different kinds of gifts, but the same Spirit," Paul wrote in 1 Corinthians 12:4-6. "There are different kinds of service, but the same Lord. There are different kinds of working, but the same God works all of them in all [people]."

As you learn (or improve) the skill of leading a small group, my prayer is that you discover the joy and fulfillment of being used by God. And if this little book assists you in that task, I can say along with Paul that my joy will be complete.

WHAT IS A "SMALL GROUP"?

Usually composed of anywhere between three and eight students, small groups typically break down into three types.

• The "Let's break up and explore this question for five minutes" small group

This is the informal, spontaneous small group you form in order to get kids sharing their thoughts on a topic or lesson. Its life span is typically five to 10 minutes, or perhaps as long as a weekend retreat. Its purpose: a one-time, quick use only — a good introduction to small groups for kids who've never experienced them.

The small Sunday school class or Bible study group

This type of small group is more for study and instruction than relationship building. And unlike the first type, this small group is ongoing — its life span can be several months to several years. Significant preparation is required for the leader of this type of small group.

The accountability/discipleship small group

This small group tends to be the most intimate of the three, and is more for relationship building, accountability, and discipling than study or instruction. Like the Bible study group, this small group is ongoing, with a life that can span several months or even years. (With this type of group, the longer the better.) If an accountability group includes a Bible study, the emphasis is on application rather than interpretation. The goal of this type of group is to build deeper relationships among the kids and facilitating adult — and to help them all live out God's Word in their lives.

14

Okay, time to grab a pen and think

about your small group—or the one you will soon lead—and jot down responses to these questions:

1. Which of these three small group types is yours most like? Or is yours a hybrid?

   small sunday school class

2. What are some goals for your small group?

   Knowledge

3. What is the anticipated life span of your small group?

   4 YRS

4. Where do you meet?

   sunday school

5. What are some of the difficulties in leading this small group?

   Attention span

WHY SMALL GROUPS?

○ **Small groups help you build closer relationships with your students.**

Think back on your own faith journey, your own spiritual history. What do you remember of the weekly meetings you may have gone to, or the talks you heard there? Chances are, not much. What a person *does* tend to remember are the relationships. And it's what happened in those relationships that helped your faith grow.

Small groups are a natural way to build significant relationships between kids and caring adults—like you. It's in a small group that you can learn more about who they really are, and what their relationships with God are like. When you lead a small group, you get involved more intimately with fewer kids—and have a deeper influence on them.

In fact, small groups help counteract the isolating "bigness" of our culture. They provide much needed context of healthy community where kids learn more about God, themselves, and each other—and where they will form meaningful relationships that will shape them for the rest of their lives.

o **Small groups provide community and friendship.**

The redefinition, regrouping, and mobility of family structures that's been evolving for the last two or three decades means, among other things, that fewer and fewer kids have a traditional community or nearby extended family to grow up with. So teenagers find their community in other places, in other ways — and not all of them healthy. What they need is a community that will support them. A place, to borrow the lyrics to the "Cheers" theme song, where everybody knows their name. The church can provide this through small groups.

• Small groups worked for the early church, and they continue to work today.

The idea behind small groups isn't new. (See Acts 2:42-47 for a description of first-century small groups.) Yet small groups continue to play a big part in the growth and development of the church. With over 40 percent of the U.S. population involved in some type of small group, religious or otherwise, it's a proven medium for effectively getting people to come together. Small-group leadership is a worthwhile skill to develop in Christian education.

HELP! i'm a small-grou leader!

Small groups help kids process and act on what they learn.

Communication is a two-way process — you speak, and they hear. Both are essential for communication. You may remember one of Gary Larson's "Far Side" strips: the first frame is what we say to dogs, in which the human says to the dog, "Ginger, I want you to stay out of the trash, understand? Stay out of the trash. OK, Ginger?" The next frame, what they hear: "Ginger, blah, blah, blah, blah, blah, blah, blah, Ginger."

Just what *do* kids hear during the average Sunday school lesson? Meeting in small groups helps

HELP! i'm a
small-group

20

you discover what it is they're hearing—and helps you more effectively teach God's Word by letting them discover the meaning for themselves.

leader!

HOW TO PUT SMALL GROUPS TOGETHER

Most youth groups are divided into *small* groups in one of three general ways.

○ Grade-level groups

Dividing them by grade level puts kids together with peers of the same age and, generally, a similar maturity level. This tends to make discussions in grade-level groups more relevant to more of the kids. It also helps inhibit the formation of cliques, because kids are brought together into a group because of their age instead of any existing friendships with others in the group.

○ Just-guys, just-girls groups

Same-sex small groups are usually best if you want more intimacy and deeper sharing than you'd get otherwise. Most junior and senior highers are dealing with their sexuality in such a profound way that it can be distracting to have members of the opposite sex in their group.

And if you organize your small groups this way, it's fun now and then to get together to plan group dates and activities (see "10 Ideas for Building Community in Your Small Group" on page 106).

HELP! i'm a

o Neighborhood or school groups

If you're in a church or parachurch organization that draws kids from several different areas or schools, think about dividing your kids into groups by region, neighborhood, school, or community. This way you can meet in homes—definitely a more relaxed environment than most church youth rooms. This small-group organization also helps kids build closer friendships with other Christians who attend their school or live in their neighborhood, thereby giving them more support for living out their faith.

leader!

small-group leader!

However you divide your groups,

mix it up every once in a while to give kids a different perspective. Variety adds to their small-group experience—and it periodically gives you, too, a new set of faces and personalities to lead in discussion and study.

HOW NOT TO LEAD A SMALL GROUP

Yes, you can become a better small-group leader by observing what makes a *poor* small-group leader. Here are five common mistakes to avoid when leading a small group.

Too Talkative

This leader is usually earnest and well meaning in his efforts to provide good leadership, but he doesn't give his students enough chances to talk. He typically begins his small group with a long introduction, and then proceeds to tell lots of personal illustrations. When he *does* finally ask a question, he doesn't wait long enough for a response. Or if students do begin to get a first word in edgewise,

...which reminds me of something else God did for me, I was ten at the time...

he'll interrupt them and, in his enthusiasm, answer the question himself. This so-called discussion quickly turns into a lecture, and students end up listening to their leader's thoughts rather than sharing their own.

Questions for reflection:

1. Circle one: I always / sometimes / never struggle with talking too much as I lead my small group.

2. Is there anything in the description of Too Talkative that especially steps on your toes?

   not wating long enough

3. Okay, so you're not tempted to talk too much as you lead your small group. Yet have you ever been in a group with a too talkative leader? What effect did it have on the group?

   sleep, irritation

4. What are some practical things you can do to avoid talking too much when you lead your small group? *?*

∘Insecure

She wants so badly to be liked by her students, she
has a hard time asserting her leadership. When a
controversial topic surfaces, she
waits to see what the kids think
before giving her opinion.
Ironically, the insecure small-
group leader usually begins being
popular with her students, but is
ultimately disrespected.
Adolescents want and need guid-
ance. In the long run they'll value
the risk their
leader takes to
speak the truth—
however unpopu-
lar it may be.

Questions for reflection:

1. Circle one: I always / sometimes / never struggle with feeling insecure as I lead my small group.

2. Is there anything in the description of Insecure that especially steps on your toes?

being popular

3. If you don't struggle with feeling insecure in your leadership, have you ever been led by someone who did? What effect did it have on the group?

4. What are some practical things you can do to make you feel more secure as you lead your small group?

○ Unprepared

She walks in late and, once she begins, you can tell she's winging it. Hasn't spent 15 minutes preparing for this small group. She's not good remembering names and tries to cover up this fact with her enthusiasm and friendliness. The unprepared leader is often very relational and charismatic, so she gets away with inadequate preparation. The kids may forgive her, but her casual (or downright lazy) approach to preparation eventually spills over to the students, who will follow her lead.

Questions for reflection:

1. Circle one: ~~I always~~ / sometimes / never struggle with unpreparedness in my small group.

2. Is there anything in the description of Unprepared that especially steps on your toes?

hasn't spent 15 min preparing

3. Good for you if you come prepared to most of your small-group meetings! But have you ever been in a group with a consistently unprepared leader? What effect did it have on the group?

scattered

4. What are some practical things you can do to consistently be prepared for leading your small group?

Always study

○ Inflexible

Despite the fact that he was recruited to lead a small group, he lacks either the knowledge, experience, or sensitivity to discern what the kids need. He prepares his Bible study immaculately—and during the meeting doesn't veer from it one inch. The kids may want—may *need*—to talk about something else, but the inflexible small-group leader has an agenda to follow and a schedule to keep. An inflexible leader is good at following directions, but may be a little dense when it comes to discerning when it's time to adjust the Bible study—or postpone it altogether—and let kids talk about what is unusually urgent for them at the moment.

Questions for reflection:

1. Circle one: I always / sometimes / never struggle with being inflexible as I lead my small group.

2. Is there anything in the description of Inflexible that especially steps on your toes?

schedule

3. If you don't struggle with this leadership style, have you ever been in a group with an inflexible leader? What effect did it have on the group?

oppressive

4. What are some practical things you can do to stay reasonably flexible as you lead your small group?

build in time

HELP! i'm a
small-group
leader!

◦ Walked On

This leader usually has good intentions but little (if any) control over his group. His kids don't think twice about interrupting him and each other. They don't follow directions. They consequently accomplish nothing when they meet as a group. Whenever he hints at asserting his leadership, the kids laugh at him or ignore him. They know they can get away with it. The worst news, though, is that the longer this pattern continues, the more difficult it is to change.

Questions for reflection:

1. Circle one: I always / sometimes / never am walked on by students in my small group.

2. Is there anything in the description of Walked On that fits your small-group leadership style?

   the get away with it

3. Good for you if you can keep the members of your small group respectful of and attentive to each other. But have you ever been in a small group with a walked-on leader? What effect did it have on the group?

   out of control

4. What are some practical things you can do to stay flexible, kind, but appropriately firm as a small-group leader?

STARTING A DISCUSSION—AND KEEPING IT GOING

Consider these 10 tips for creating a comfortable small-group atmosphere—a necessary quality if you want all students to enjoy participating.

1. Encourage your students to verbalize their views and feelings, however unorthodox they may be.

Nothing stifles a discussion faster than when kids don't feel safe to say what they feel. If they get shot down by you or the members of the group, they'll be less likely to share next time. Kids new to the faith (or not yet in the faith) need a place to process their religious views without feeling self-conscious.

roup leader!

As a senior in high school I had some views shaped by a Christian Science background. And because I was allowed to share those views in a small group (without feeling stupid), I was able to reshape them in the course of discussion and Bible study. If the group hadn't been open to my opinions, my defensiveness could have created a barrier to further growth and maturity. Instead, this small group became an important part of my spiritual development.

Small groups should be a place where adolescents can be honest about what they're thinking and feeling—no matter what's on their minds. What students discover for themselves remains with them far longer than anything you tell them. Be slow to correct them, but instead let them think through their own responses. This is usually a better way for them to make genuine and lasting discoveries about God.

2. Be grateful for every answer.

Yes, *every* answer. Leaders can also stifle discussion
by inadvertently making students feel silly or
dumb about their responses and comments. Your
job is to create a safe place for kids to say whatever
they want—and be appreciated for it. Sure, if you
work with seventh grade males, you'll need to gently redirect the tangents that pop up every three
minutes. (Hmmm...seventh grade males...did we
say *gently*?) But it's generally better to encourage
freedom of speech.

To encourage this freedom, set a ground rule
that when someone is speaking, they have the

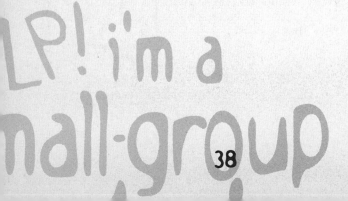

floor — they should not be interrupted. When they are finished, anyone else may share their opinion as long as it is not critical of anyone in the group. To help students visualize this, pass around an object that one must hold in order to have the floor.

As students feel free to say what's on their minds, they will trust you and the group (and themselves) more, creating an environment for growth.

CLAP! CLAP! CLAP!

3. Don't be satisfied with the first response to your question.

Avoid setting a question-answer-question-answer pattern. Here's a better way to start a discussion: ask for several responses to your question, then provoke the speakers to dialogue with each other. That is, move them from merely answering toward discussing or conversing—with each other, not just with you.

Start the ball rolling in this direction by asking "Why do you think that?" and "What do the rest of you think?" Don't let it rest with the first answer, but encourage discussion. Draw students out by asking questions whose answers aren't so obvious.

Occasionally play devil's advocate and question students' responses—especially if they tend to give typical "church answers." Challenge church kids to go deeper and examine their own faith, rather than live the one that's been handed down to them.

4. Keep the discussion moving.

A Bible study that does not move along at a good pace tends to get dull. This often occurs when one or two students monopolize the discussion while the rest of the group nods off. Be aware of this and quickly move on to the next question. If you have a student who genuinely wants to further discuss an issue, set up an appointment at a later time. Avoid turning discussion time into a one-on-one dialogue that everyone else observes.

If you must choose your evils, choose frustrated students who wanted to spend more time resolving an issue—not bored students who have been

gradually distancing themselves from the discussion. Jesus, you remember, often left questions unanswered. It helps people think for themselves. Your students will learn more by being frustrated with an unresolved issue, than being satisfied with a thorough response.

5. Be alert to the individuals in your group.

Be aware of what's going on with your kids as they come to your small group. In fact, you may want to reserve the first few minutes of your time for small talk and sharing. Kids can catch up with each other before (instead of during) your small-group time.

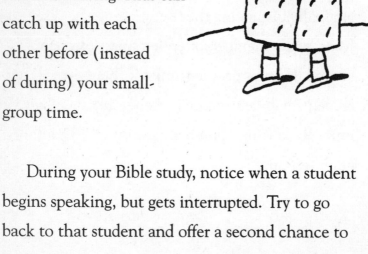

During your Bible study, notice when a student begins speaking, but gets interrupted. Try to go back to that student and offer a second chance to share. Look beyond those who are monopolizing the discussion, and deliberately ask other, quieter students for their responses. Encourage their participation without putting them on the spot, and affirm them regardless of their contribution to the discussion.

You'll never stop some personalities from standing out in your group; others will insist on staying in the background. That's okay. Just be observant. If a student is clearly preoccupied, she may need to talk before she can fully participate in your Bible study. Your goal is to make every student feel that they are an important member of your group, and this means discerning when to lay aside your agenda for a group member who needs your support.

HELP! i'm a small
group le

6. Don't be afraid of silence.

If your question gets no immediate response from a student, don't feel you have to jump in and answer it yourself. Let the question linger in the air for a while. And let kids know that you're comfortable with the silence and willing to wait for discussion to begin.

Two things will happen if you jump in right away. First, you will interrupt any thoughtful reflection, and second, kids will learn that you'll always rescue them, setting a pattern that is hard to break. Small groups are for students to struggle with their thoughts. You, as the leader, need to provide the time and space to facilitate that.

Silence is often an answer in itself—or can be a necessary prelude to a deeply felt response. Of course, if every question you ask is met with prolonged silence, you may need to take a hard look at the kinds of questions you're asking. (More on asking good questions in "Ask Questions That Get Responses" on page 60.)

7. Turn difficult questions back to the group.

If you're intimidated by a student with a tough question, join the crowd. Yet that very question, tough as it may be, can give you a chance to get a lively discussion going. Don't think you have to try to answer it—try turning the question back to the group instead: "Good question, Dan. What do the rest of you think?" (It also gets you off the hook if you don't know the answer.)

Help your students examine what they believe by constantly asking for their thoughts and opinions. You may get some wild answers, but the students will be encouraged to think for themselves rather than look to you for answers. You will also benefit by understanding where your kids are in their spiritual journey.

If a question remains unresolved, now and then challenge your small group to find the answer by your next meeting. (A prize can add some motivation here.) Give suggestions for where they might begin researching (a book, a person to ask), and be prepared to search for the answer yourself.

So what do you think about that?

8. Let your group self-correct its tangents.

The technique of turning a question back to the group is also a remedy for wild tangents. Don't just tell the student that he or she is wrong (and possibly stifle a student's participation)—ask instead, "What do the rest of you think?" Chances are as students give their input, the group will correct itself. This also encourages your students to dialogue with each other instead of directing their dialogue toward you.

People grow in their understanding of the faith as they refine their ideas in dialogue with other Christians. In the small-group setting, students work out their theology best by discussing their thoughts with each other and with you. As a leader, refrain from giving the right answers, for in

this way you create a greater opportunity for learning.

According to Edgar Dale's "cone of learning," students retain far more knowledge from a discussion than from merely listening. Nevertheless, I have observed countless small-group leaders turn their Bible studies into more of a lecture than a discussion. Small groups should be a place for your students to process their own thoughts rather than listen to yours.

HELP! i'm a

9. Stay flexible to the group's needs.

Sooner or later (usually sooner), a student will come to her small-group meeting with a specific, significant, and often immediate concern that needs to be addressed in the context of the small group. It may be an unresolved conflict between group members, a friend (perhaps there that night) who wants to know more about Christ, a recent death, an impending divorce. Now is the time to put aside your agenda and deal with the issue.

This shouldn't happen every week, however. If it does, you can either spend more time with individual students outside your group time, or lengthen your meeting to include a longer sharing time. If students know they will have time to share what's on their hearts, they will be more able to focus on your Bible study. Leading a small group requires the judgment to decide when an issue is sufficiently critical that you need to deal with it instead of leading your planned discussion.

Staying flexible also means recognizing when your group needs a change. Use creative, active Bible studies and/or various activities and challenges to keep your group fresh and exciting. Try the Creative Bible Lessons series (published by Youth Specialties) for new ideas to help the Scriptures come alive. Your group may also benefit from time together outside of your regular meeting—for fun as well as service. This gives them the opportunity to put faith in action as they grow closer together. (For specific ideas see "10 Ideas for Building Community in Your Small Group" on page 106.)

small-group leader!

10. Be prepared to learn from your group.

This is sometimes the best part of leading a small group. Your weekly preparation (which challenges you to stay grounded in the Word) as well as the students' feedback can profoundly influence your own spiritual development. As a leader you are essentially asking students to "Follow my example, as I follow the example of Christ" (1 Corinthians 11:1). But as this verse suggests, it's the reality of Christ in your life, not your own personal perfection, that will have the biggest impact on your students.

Sometimes kids experience the reality of Christ better by observing your struggles rather than your strengths. Students are greatly impacted by the leader who takes the risk and becomes vulnerable,

demonstrating their own need for the love and grace of Jesus Christ. Of course you will need to discern what is appropriate for sharing with your small group; but the more your kids see that you struggle too, the less intimidated they will be by your spirituality and leadership.

Ministry breeds maturity, and your ministry as a small-group leader will help you to "become mature, attaining to the whole measure of the fullness of Christ" (Ephesians 4:13). As you nurture and care for the spiritual lives of your students, you will inevitably grow in your own spiritual life—becoming more the person Christ intends you to be. You will say with Paul, "Not that I have already obtained all this, or have already been made perfect, but I press on to take hold of that for which Christ Jesus took hold of me" (Philippians 3:12). Perhaps this is the greatest gift you can give your students.

THE IMPORTANCE OF CONFIDENTIALITY

If you want kids to feel safe enough to share themselves deeply with others in their small group, then it's up to you to establish trust and confidentiality. Some small-group leaders use a written or verbal agreement, committing signers to the principle that whatever is shared in the group stays in the group. They don't tell their parents or their boyfriends the particulars of what they hear in their small group, and you don't tell your spouse.

If what you hear from a student during a meeting of your small group makes you think that a one-

HELP! i'm a
small-group

to-one talk would be appreciated or helpful, it is no breach of confidence for you to meet with the student over a hamburger later that week and talk personally.

leader!

◦Know the law.

There are critical exceptions to this rule, of course. If a student confides anything that even hints at physical or sexual abuse, you are *required* by some state laws to report that information to law-enforcement authorities. Know ahead of time what course of action is required of you by your supervisor, your church, and your state if you hear inklings of self-destructive or addictive behavior from students in your small group. At least you will probably talk to such students privately, recommending professional

ELP! i'm a
small-group
leader!

help with specific names and numbers. Keep an up-to-date list of local referral agencies for this purpose.

If confidence is broken in your group, deal with it immediately so that trust can be re-established. Meet privately with the group members who were involved, either individually or together, depending on circumstances. Your goal is to help kids learn when to share personal information with a third party, and when to keep such information to oneself.

ASK QUESTIONS THAT GET RESPONSES

Whether they're personal questions, topical questions, or Bible study questions, how you ask them can make the difference between lively small-group discussions and dead ones.

○ Avoid yes or no questions.

Stay away from questions that begin with "Is there...?," "Are they...?" or "Do you think...?" With a yes or no, your discussion could end right there. Instead ask more *why* questions.

In small-group ministry it is your questions rather than your answers that make your small group a good one. So it's worth the extra time to find questions to provoke good group discussion. If

you write your own material, look at some different Bible studies or questionnaires to learn how to craft good questions. If you use a curriculum written by someone else, rewrite the questions that seem obvious or boring.

Another suggestion: run your questions by a friend before your small-group meeting to see if they're dead-end yes-or-no questions, or if they provoke exploration, opinions, and discussion. Sometimes it's difficult to tell, and it's better to find out *before* your discussion rather than during.

∘ Don't ask questions that assume an answer.

Asking "How does Jesus show his anger in this passage?" assumes that a) Jesus is angry, and b) there is a right answer you want your kids to discover. The problem with such questions is that they tell students too much without leaving stu-

ANSWER:
a) The Essenes
b) Hypostasis
c) 57 cubits
d) None of the Above

dents room to discover answers and insights themselves. Remember your goal is to invite students to explore a passage and share their own thoughts rather than being directed toward yours.

A better question: "What is Jesus feeling in this passage? Why do you think he feels this way?" This encourages kids to share their opinions, not just give the answers they think you want. They'll be led into a deeper exploration of their faith and a much more interesting discussion. (For examples of questions to ask see "100 Ready-to-Go Questions for Small-Group Bible Studies" on page 116.)

It's difficult to know if a question leads to a specific response until you ask it, so again, run the questions by a friend prior to the meeting. Or enlist the help of a student to write your questions, and use it as an opportunity for some one-on-one time with them. Depending on their maturity level, invite them to help you lead that week's small group and give another valuable opportunity for growth.

○ Write questions that are relevant to your kids.

Some good questions will spring to your mind during the meeting, but don't rely on those. Instead spend some thinking time before the meeting—about where your kids are, what their maturity level is, what in the study is particularly relevant to your students—and thoughtfully write out most of your questions.

Doing a Bible study on David and Bathsheba (2 Samuel 11)? Don't ask "What effect do you think David's sin of adultery had on his life?"—it's not nearly as relevant to kids as "What could David have done to keep from having sex with Bathsheba?" Questions like these will not only draw your kids' interest, they will help students discuss in a vicarious way how they can handle their

The People Who Brought You this Book...
invite you to discover MORE valuable youth ministry resources.

Youth Specialities has three decades of experience working alongside Christian youth workers of just about every denomination and youth-serving organization. We're here to help you, whether you're brand new to youth ministry or a veteran, whether you're a volunteer or a career youth pastor. Each year we serve over 100,000 youth workers worldwide through our training seminars, conventions, magazines, resource products, and internet Web site (www.YouthSpecialties.com).

For FREE information about ways YS can help your youth ministry, complete and return this card.

Are you: ☐ A paid youth worker   ☐ A volunteer   S=480001

Name _____

Church/Org. _____

Address ☐ Church or ☐ Home _____

City _____ State _____ Zip _____

Daytime Phone Number (_____) _____

E-Mail _____

Denomination _____ Average Weekly Church Attendance _____

The People Who Brought You this Book...
invite you to discover MORE valuable youth ministry resources.

Youth Specialities has three decades of experience working alongside Christian youth workers of just about every denomination and youth-serving organization. We're here to help you, whether you're brand new to youth ministry or a veteran, whether you're a volunteer or a career youth pastor. Each year we serve over 100,000 youth workers worldwide through our training seminars, conventions, magazines, resource products, and internet Web site (www.YouthSpecialties.com).

For FREE information about ways YS can help your youth ministry, complete and return this card.

Are you: ☐ A paid youth worker   ☐ A volunteer   S=480001

Name _____

Church/Org. _____

Address ☐ Church or ☐ Home _____

City _____ State _____ Zip _____

Daytime Phone Number (_____) _____

E-Mail _____

Denomination _____ Average Weekly Church Attendance _____

BUSINESS REPLY MAIL

FIRST-CLASS MAIL   PERMIT 268   HOLMES PA

POSTAGE WILL BE PAID BY ADDRESSEE

YOUTH SPECIALTIES
P.O. BOX 668
HOLMES, PA 19043-0668

BUSINESS REPLY MAIL

FIRST-CLASS MAIL   PERMIT 268   HOLMES PA

POSTAGE WILL BE PAID BY ADDRESSEE

YOUTH SPECIALTIES
P.O. BOX 668
HOLMES, PA 19043-0668

own sexual temptation. Kids are more apt to talk if questions clearly reflect issues in their own lives—and what they learn from the ensuing discussions will be more valuable to their spiritual journey.

Spend time getting to know your kids so that you can determine what they are interested in, and what they are ready to learn for spiritual growth. This may be your most valuable exercise in crafting your small-group questions.

◦ Learn how and when to ask direct questions

Direct questions like "Sue, is Jesus the Lord of your life?" may lead to meaningful dialogue, but only with the right people at the right time. If this is Sue's first meeting, a question like this may make it her last. Students in your group must grow in intimacy and trust before such questions are appropriate.

If this is the small group's first meeting, or you have some new students in the group, try the less threatening "How does Jesus become the Lord of your life?" and open it up to the group in general instead of directing the question to an individual. In this way your students may share without being put on the spot, and you will be able to determine where your students are spiritually. Their responses will give you something to follow up on when you're with them one-on-one.

As your small group grows in trust and openness with each other, you can gradually use more direct questions to challenge your kids personally. Some students are never asked about where they are in their faith, and it can be a tragic oversight not to give them the personal opportunity to respond to the gospel. Over time your group will learn to trust you, each other, and themselves—and they will feel safe to be more vulnerable as you continue to meet together.

◦ Ask questions that deal with feelings as well as facts.

Your goal is to engage your students' hearts as well as their minds. It's usually safer to deal with issues objectively ("What sins in St. Paul's list are teenagers at your school particularly inclined to?") rather than personally ("What sins in St. Paul's list should you give up?"). Yet the longer your small group meets, the deeper and more personal your questions can become.

A good litmus test for the intimacy of your group is the kinds of questions you feel free to ask

HELP! i'm a small-group

(and students feel free to answer). If your group has been meeting for some time and hasn't gotten very personal, you may want to evaluate why—and perhaps ask the students as well. Healthy small groups should grow in intimacy and trust, and your continual evaluation will help strengthen the effectiveness of your ministry.

The ability to craft good questions is a vital skill for effective ministry. As you peruse the New Testament, you'll discover that Jesus ministered to people more with his questions than with his answers—inviting people to find the truth for themselves. Small-group ministry allows us to spend less time telling and more time asking—more closely representing the ministry of Christ.

THREE KINDS OF BIBLE STUDY QUESTIONS TO ASK

Those three kinds are questions of observation, of interpretation, and of application.

Observation

These are questions of fact: *What does the passage say?*

Questions of observation—and their answers—ensure that kids know the plain facts of a Bible passage before launching into an interpretation of it. When Bible studies go off on tangents, it's usually because group members start interpreting the text before they have the facts.

Observation questions help you and your students carefully examine a passage and find important

details together—details individuals might miss on their
own. Your students will
discover the value of
careful reading and
reflection, and
hopefully apply
this practice in
their own study of
God's Word. This may
be an avenue through
which God begins to
reveal something they
need to see in their own lives.

So begin your Bible study with two or three
questions of fact, starting with such words as *who*,
what, *describe*, *find*, or *list*. Don't spend most of your
time on questions of observation, but by all means
start here.

Interpretation

These are questions of meaning: *What does this passage mean?*

This is the next level of questioning, in which your questions should encourage kids to share their thoughts about what they think a verse or passage means. Questions of interpretation frequently begin with the words *why, how,* or *explain.*

Such questions lead students to read and understand the Bible for themselves. If God is beginning to speak to them through their observation of a passage, your interpretation questions will allow a deeper exploration and provide a bridge to the application questions, which ultimately personalize the text.

Through interpretation questions, students combine their observations with thoughts about their observations, moving them from reading the passage to getting involved in it. Like Jesus' parables, your questions should draw students in so that they see how the passage speaks to their lives. By working through interpretation questions, students will see the truths of Scripture in relation to present-day faith and life.

HELP! i'm a small-group leader!

Application

These are questions of personal relevance: *What does this passage mean to me?*

Application questions are interpretation questions with a personal touch. They call for personal reflection rather than objective response and require a complete shift from discussion of the general meaning of the passage to a discussion of its relevance to life.

Questions of application

can be the most difficult to formulate, but they are the essential link between Bible study and your students' daily lives. Most small-group Bible study time is often spent here. The goal of application questions is for kids to find themselves in the passage you're studying, then to discover how the meaning of the text speaks to their own lives. Typical questions of application: "Which person in this story do you relate to the most? If you were with Jesus [in this passage], what would he say to you?"

This may be the most important part of your small-group Bible study, for it is through such questions that your students develop a more personal understanding of their faith and discover how to be Christians in their day-to-day world.

Beginning on page 116 is a huge list of Observation, Interpretation, and Application questions on common biblical and topical studies. Use these questions as they are, or as examples for your own Bible study questions.

You know what it's like watching the individual personalities in a small group emerge—even if the small group is a family. Your challenge as a small-group leader is to learn to work with the personalities in your small group and help all your students grow individually even as they learn to function as a group.

Here are six types of student personalities,

most of which you'll meet in a typical small group of teenagers. The aim isn't to stereotype students, but to help you anticipate common traits and character-istics you'll encounter in your small group—and then to help you find ways to minister more effec-tively to the kids.

The Talker

This is the student in your small group who never stops talking, who always has a comment for everything. You're tempted to apply duct tape, but don't—there are more productive ways to handle this student. First, position the Talker next to you when you begin your group, which reduces eye contact with her when you ask a question—and, when she interrupts someone, lets you reach over and touch her arm (usually a silent but effective cue). If you have a whole group of Talkers, you may want to try the ground rule that stipulates that the small group must circulate an object—a stuffed animal, Nerf Ball, spit wad, whatever—and that a student must possess it before speaking. This will help Talkers wait their turn.

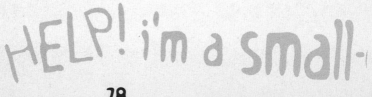

Chances are, the Talker has some natural leadership ability that you should encourage. So let her lead the small group now and then. This can help her appreciate what you endure as a leader, and she just may become more sup-portive when *you* lead.

If the problem persists, get some time alone with her and talk with her about giving others a chance to answer the questions. Help her feel that she's on your team, and that the two of you need to work together to encourage the other students to respond.

group leader!

The Thinker

This student is quieter (and usually shier) than the others, with a tendency to get drowned out by the louder personalities in your group. So bring him out more by positioning him across from you, to increase the chances of eye contact with you. You can also use the tried-and-true

method of occasionally directing questions to specific students, thereby eliciting responses from the Thinker.

If the Thinker is particularly shy, spend one-on-one time with him to discover what he's interested in—and so you can create the kinds of questions that will bring him into the discussion. Use the positive reinforcement of affirming him on those occasions when he actually *does* respond publicly. And when he lapses back into silence, don't interpret that silence as something that needs to be fixed. Some kids just learn best by listening and watching—and there's a good chance he's one of them.

The Church Kid

This kid has already spent more hours in this church
than you probably have. She's progressed from the
church nursery to the high school room in the
course of her 14 or 15 years there. She consequently
knows more about the Bible than any other kid in
youth group, not to mention her small group. Of
course, her knowledge may or may not indicate spiritual depth.

Church Kids can be the hardest to reach
because they've heard it all, and therefore feel they
have nothing to learn. One way to challenge them
is by not being satisfied with pat answers. Always
ask *why*. Or play devil's advocate by countering her
squeaky-clean, correct answers with provocative
arguments from the other side of the issue. Such

strategies usually force a
Church Kid to think
more deeply about her
answers instead of just rattling them off.

Ask her help you cre-
ate questions for a Bible
study—or even let her
lead the small group
once in a while. In any case,
avoid asking questions that
invite a "right" answer.
Opt instead for questions
that leave room for a variety
of valid responses.

The Distracter

This is the student who can't sit still and ends up distracting everyone in your small group—including you. Rather than constantly stifling him, direct his energy toward productive ends: ask him to help you pass out Bibles, set up chairs, serve refreshments. Or (and

GROUP ACTIVITY

ADOPT-A-PERSONALITY ROLE PLAY

Are you working through this handbook together with other small-group leaders? Then try this exercise that introduces you all to common personalities of kids in your small groups.

this is good advice for all small groups, with or without Distracters) do some active-learning experiences with your small group—like object lessons or field trips—instead of just sitting and talking week after week.

You may better understand this student (and where his energy comes from) if you get together with him outside of your small group. Even a Distracter can be good for your small group, if only because he doesn't let you get by with boring Bible studies. (Remember *that* when you're tempted to quit.) Really—your leadership skills will be sharpened as you find ways to engage him as well as the tranquil students in your lesson.

You'll need pens, index cards, and the section "100 Ready-to-Go Questions for Small-Group Bible Studies" in this booklet (which starts on page 116). If your group is large, break up into smaller groups of five to eight. Designate a leader in your group (let the leader be the one with the most experience working with kids), who numbers the index cards 1 through 6, then distributes them to members of the group. (You don't have to use all six cards.) Once you get your card,

CONTINUED ON NEXT PAGE

The Debater

She irritates you by challenging every point you (or anyone else) tries to make. Sure, she brings a creative energy to the group sometimes—but she often stifles the other kids by making them feel too threatened to voice their opinions or feelings.

ROLE PLAY CONTINUED

match the number on the card with the teenage personality listed below—and assume that personality! Don't tell the group which personality you're playing. Let them try to guess.

1. THE TALKER—never stops talking, always a comment for everything
2. THE THINKER—extremely shy, doesn't speak, keeps to himself
3. THE CHURCH KID—grew up in the church, has all the right answers, little spiritual depth
4. THE DISTRACTER—can't sit still, distracts everyone in the group

Deal with the Debater by establishing ground rules for your small group, the first (and perhaps the only) being: *It's okay to disagree with opinions, but it is inappropriate to attack or put down other small-group members if their opinions differ from yours.* A second ground rule may be that only one person may talk at a time. Ground rules like these help make a Debater's criticism less caustic and restrains her from interrupting others in order to make her point.

The good news: once Debaters understand and abide by such rules, their input can actually enliven your discussion. Just remember that your goal is to direct, not stifle, their participation.

5. THE DEBATER—always playing devil's advocate, argues every point
6. THE CRISIS PRODUCER—always in a crisis, has a personal illustration for everything

NOW, using one of the Bible studies from the section "100 Ready-to-Go Questions for Small-Group Bible Studies," act out a small-group Bible study for five minutes or so.

WHEN YOU'RE DONE, all of you take a guess about which personality each of you assumed. Share any ideas you have for how to work with these personalities. Then, beginning on page 76, read through the descriptions of each of the personalities—which include suggestions for working with them.

The Crisis Producer

This student is in perpetual crisis—and lets your small group know about it every meeting. He's often self-absorbed and therefore unable to participate in the discussion, except when it's focused on him. So get together with him before your small group begins in order to talk through his problems with just you instead of

bringing them to the small group. (Lucky you.) Or begin your small-group discussion with the assurance that everyone will have a chance to share problems, prayer requests, etc., at the end of the group. This helps members—and especially Crisis Producers—stay focused on your Bible study.

Whatever your strategy with your Crisis Producer, your long goal is to help him see past his crises to some solutions, and then to participate in your small group without having to constantly bring the focus back to himself.

What about a student who raises a legitimate crisis during the discussion? Be flexible enough to postpone your study and deal with the issue at hand.

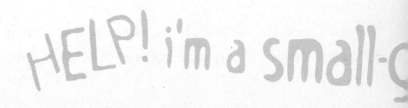

YOU CAN HELP YOUR KIDS LEARN TO PRAY

Praying out loud can be intimidating, especially for kids who are new to the faith. Yet praying together can be one of the most encouraging and bonding experiences for your group. As the small-group leader you will have the privilege of leading your students in prayer—possibly for the very first time—helping them learn to talk (and listen) to God. Here are some tips:

1. Encourage students to pray by modeling rather than by instruction.

Like most adults, students tend to believe that praying requires a language or tone of voice they never use in everyday life—usually deep and low with lots of thees and thous. Often it's because of what they've observed in church. Your own example will demonstrate that this formality is not necessary; they can just pray in their own words.

When Jesus taught on prayer, he used the Lord's prayer as a guide. He encouraged them (and us) to pray simply and directly, instead of babbling on with many words (Matthew 6:7). Jesus often addressed God as Abba, which, when translated from the Greek, means Daddy rather than Father. God desires for us to be straightforward and address him intimately.

You may be comfortable with a certain style of praying, and that's fine—the point here is to show your students that their prayers can be personal and simple. So if you pray simply and naturally with your students, they'll see that it's okay to pray similarly—in and outside of your group.

2. Make it clear that prayer is talking (or listening) to God, not to each other.

Some kids feel self-conscious praying publicly for the first time, even if it's in a small group. So remind them before you pray that they aren't speaking to each other, but to God.

One way to alleviate their self-consciousness is by praying together in one-word prayers, or with short phrases of thanksgiving. Have them go through the alphabet naming things they're thankful for that begin with each letter. Or start a sentence and have your students finish it: "God, I am grateful for...", or "Please help me to..." or (my personal favorite) "My youth leader is great because..."

Eventually your students will become comfortable talking to God and will be able to spend longer periods of time praying together. The experience of praying in a group will be a first for many of your kids, and it will be their initial step in learning to more regularly communicate with God.

3. Don't give advice or pass gossip and call it praying.

Teenagers as well as adults are capable of verbalizing information that shouldn't be verbalized, intentionally or otherwise, in the form of a prayer: "Please God, help Bill stop partying," or "Give Sue wisdom as she deals with her pregnancy." Bill and Sue may need prayer, but they don't need people talking about them.

whoa! Brittany actually said that?!

Cut off this tendency early by encouraging your students to pray for their friends anonymously. (After all, God knows who they are.) This will help your students pray more and more for the benefit of God's ears rather than each other's.

If your kids want to pray specifically, let them start with their own weaknesses and dilemmas rather than broadcast a friend's failings to the rest of the group. (This is good advice for adult small groups as well.) Often your 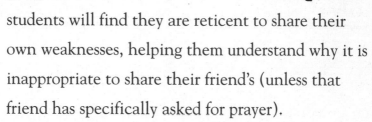 students will find they are reticent to share their own weaknesses, helping them understand why it is inappropriate to share their friend's (unless that friend has specifically asked for prayer).

The more you pray for each other, the closer your group becomes. Students are encouraged by God's answers in their own lives and in the lives of others, which can strengthen and build up their faith.

4. Don't spend your prayer time talking about what to pray for.

This is an easy trap for a small group to fall into. With 15 minutes left to pray, you spend 12-13 minutes sharing prayer requests, and suddenly realize you've got two minutes left to pray. Unfortunately when this becomes a pattern, your group ends up spending far more time sharing concerns than praying them.

Occasionally divide your group into pairs so they can share their requests and pray together. This will provide the time needed for individuals to share *and* be prayed for. It also gives shy students the opportunity to still pray out loud. Though praying together may seem awkward or scary at first, praying out loud with other

PRAYER LIST

Christians will bind them together in a unique way.

Most importantly, use your prayer time to *do it*, not to talk about it. If you're short with time, cut to the chase—dispense altogether with exchanging prayer requests, ask your kids to pray their concerns to God, and assure them the group will pray along with them. Use your own actions as a small-group leader to emphasize the importance of prayer.

5. Relish silence.

Quiet moments during public prayer make
some students (and leaders)
feel awkward or uncom-
fortable. Students
will generally
follow your
lead. If you are
comfortable with
the silence, they
will be, too. And
you will commu-
nicate through
your actions that
you are focused
on being in the
presence of God.

Suggest to students before you pray that they use the silent intervals for silent prayer. Some students will be more comfortable with this anyway. Kids today have so few opportunities to be quiet—it could be a valuable time for your group. And spending time in silence can often be the most meaningful part of prayer because you give God space to speak.

Don't always feel like you have to fill the silence with words—though it will be tempting if you sense the restlessness of your students. It's good for your group to learn that prayer is more than rattling off a list of requests. By learning to relish the silence, your students will learn that prayer is as much listening to God as it is talking to him.

6. Assure students that they can pray freely.

You cultivate adolescents' growth in prayer as much by your restraint as by your instruction. There will be times when you'll feel like correcting your students' prayers, but it's far more beneficial for them to develop confidence in prayer, rather than "saying it right." Your students' prayers can be refreshing for your own prayer life, often providing humor and delight for you as they inevitably do for God. As Jesus reminded his disciples to "let the little children come to me and do not hinder them" (Matthew 19:14), so he reminds us as youth workers to let our kids approach the throne with confidence and grace.

If a student voices some particularly wretched theology during prayer, don't correct her—at least not at that meeting. Make a mental note to find an opportunity in the future, maybe during some one-on-one time, or through a lesson or Bible study on prayer. Try not to correct your students at the time they make the mistake, because even if they laugh it off, it may inhibit them from praying freely in the future. These kinds of mistakes usually work themselves out in time as kids learn more and grow in their faith. The more experience they have praying, the more comfortable they will become—and the more intimate their relationship with God will be.

HELP! i'm a sn

7. Keep a prayer journal for your group.

Demonstrate the value of prayer by keeping a journal of your small group's prayer requests. Your group will be encouraged to see God's faithfulness. Often the concerns of yesterday are forgotten or replaced by the more pressing concerns of today, and we lose the opportunity to celebrate God's goodness.

Every now and then review all the ways God has answered students' prayers—or how God has apparently not answered them yet. Talk about whether or not his answers were what they expected. It will provide an illustration on the purpose of prayer and how much it changes our perspective to watch the ways God works in our lives. Keeping a prayer journal helps your students see how God is at work in their lives—and although his answers aren't always what we expect, they're usually what we need. Kids will witness how living and active God is in their lives.

As your students chart their prayers over time, they will also see how their prayers change as they mature. Like a growth measurement penciled on a wall, your journal will chart kids' spiritual growth— and give a written testimony of the power of God. Your students will be encouraged to keep praying, and see that God is worthy of their trust.

8. Assign new prayer partners each week for ongoing support.

Help kids learn to pray for each other outside of the meetings by assigning prayer partners for the week. This will provide ongoing support between small-group meetings, help them develop (and deepen) their personal prayer times, and build closer friendships within your group.

As students uphold one another in prayer, they will learn to care for each other— and learn the value of Christian support. God did not design us to live the Christian life alone, and the sooner kids understand this, the more likely they will solicit this kind of support in the future. Romans 12:4, 5 says, "Just as each of us has one body with many members, and these members do not all have the same function, so in Christ we who are many form one body, and each member belongs to all the others." Paul draws on the analogy of the human body to show that Christian support is not an option, but an integral part of our faith.

Your students will not always have your small group to encourage them—but if they realize their need for support through the experience of your group, you will have made an invaluable contribution to their lives. They will leave your group in search of other groups to be a part of, and this will keep them grounded in the faith.

10 IDEAS FOR BUILDING COMMUNITY IN YOUR SMALL GROUP

1. A time of affirmation

Plan a time when your small group will take some time affirming each individual. You may want to limit or even out the number of affirmations each student gets with this ground rule: only two people can say something about a student. This is a great way for students to get the positive reinforcement they need.

2. Sneaky sticky notes

Have some fun encouraging each other! Suggest to your students that they write affirming remarks to another group member on Post-It notes, then sneak them to each other during the week. Encourage creativity—they can sneak the notes into lockers, textbooks, car dashboards, bathroom mirrors, etc.

3. The morning-after accountability

Your students can hold each other accountable by pairing off and calling each other the morning after a party or date. Knowing they'll be getting that phone call just might make a differ-ence in their behavior the night before!

4. The progressive dinner

Get to know more about your students—and their families—by having a several-course dinner, each course served at a different student's home. Add spice to this classic by giving your students not directions to the next house, but clues (in the form of a scavenger hunt, if you want to get extravagant) that they must figure out as a group.

small-group leader!

5. Lady and the tramp night

Time to try a creative group date? In this version
the young men host the young women for a
spaghetti dinner. Girls dress up for the night, the
guys dress down—and only the girls get silverware.
The evening ends with a viewing of Disney's *Lady
and the Tramp*.

6. Ceremony of reconciliation

This is a time in your small group for friends to apologize to or confront each other—either verbally or in writing. First read Matthew 5:23-24, give them a time of silence for God to speak to them (an extended time, if appropriate). *Then* begin the reconciliations, in whatever form they take.

7. Self-addressed commitments

Take advantage of the closing session of a camp or retreat to ask your small-group members to privately write down one decision they can commit to, seal it in an envelope, address it to their home, and give it to you. Sometime during the next week or two, you mail all the envelopes to the students as a reminder of their decisions.

8. Rent-a-parent

After you clear the idea with parents of your small-group members, suggest to the students that if any of them need a mother or father figure for whatever reason—recognition at a school assembly, a father-daughter or mother-son activity, to attend a game or performance a kid is in, or just to get a ride with or hang out with or have dinner with—they can share another student's parent for that purpose.

HELP! i'm a small-grou leader!

9. Adopt-a-family

Your small group adopts a family in the church or community who is having a tough time, whether financially, emotionally, or domestically. You could write notes, leave a care package on their doorstep, cook a meal, etc. It's a great way for a small group to acquire the skill of serving.

HELP! i'm a small-group leader!

10. Sponsor a child through Compassion International

For $24 a month—that's about a buck per week per student—your small group can feed, clothe, and educate a child. Call Compassion International at 800-336-7676, or write them at P.O. Box 7000, Colorado Springs, CO 80933-7000. Or check out other relief organizations, like World Vision (P.O. Box 9716, Federal Way, WA 98063-9716; 800-777-5777).

100 READY-TO-GO QUESTIONS FOR SMALL-GROUP BIBLE STUDIES

Here are questions for 10 common small-group Bible studies—five Bible text studies (two from Genesis, a Psalm, and selections from the Gospel of Mark and the letter to the Ephesians) and five topical studies (friendship; family; self-image; love, sex, and dating; and sharing your faith). Questions are organized according to whether they're questions of observation, interpretation, or application. (See pages 70-75 for how to use these three kinds of questions.)

CREATION
GENESIS 1, 2

Observation

1. Look at Genesis 1:1. What questions does it answer about creation? What questions doesn't it answer?

2. Read chapter 1, verses 3, 6, 9, 14, 20, 24, and 26. What similarities do you find in these verses? What information do they give us about how God created the world?

3. What does chapter 1, verses 26-28 say about how we were created? What does Genesis 2:4-24 say? What do these passages have in common? How are they different?

Interpretation

4. How is God introduced to us in the Bible? Why do you think he is introduced this way?

5. Chapter 1, verses 26-27 says that God created human beings in his image and likeness. What do you think this means? How are we like God?

6. What do you think it means for human beings to rule over creation? How do you think we're doing?

Application

7. How does this account of creation compare with what you've learned about the beginning of the world? In what ways is it compatible? In what ways is it incompatible?

8. What evidence do you see (if any) that God created the world?

9. What evidence do you see (if any) that God created you?

10. How do you see God's image reflected in your life? In what ways are you like God? In what ways are you different from God?

ABRAHAM
GENESIS 12

Observation

1. What does God say the first time he speaks to Abraham (verses 1-2)? What promise does he make? What does Abraham have to do to receive this promise?

2. What is Abraham's response to God (verse 4)? Does he say anything? What does he do?

3. What does Abram do when he gets to Egypt (verses 10-13)? What is the result (verse 17)?

Interpretation

4. How do you think Abraham felt when God spoke to him (verses 1-2)? What does his response tell you about their relationship?

5. What reasons would Abraham have for not going where God told him to? What reasons would he have for going?

6. After taking that initial step of faith, why do you think Abraham lied about Sarah once he got there? Does that change your perspective of Abraham? Why or why not?

Application

7. How do you relate to Abraham in this passage? Do you relate to him more when he follows God or when he lies about Sarah—or both? Why?

8. What is the biggest step of faith you've ever taken? What was the result?

9. How would you rank your faith on a scale of 1 to 10 (1 being no faith and 10 being a faultless faith)? Why?

10. What (if anything) do you need from God to increase your faith? What (if anything) do you need to do to increase your faith?

HELP! i'm a small-group leader!

PSALM 27

Observation

1. What does David say about God in verses 1-2? What questions does he ask?

2. What does David ask of the Lord (verse 4)? What does he say the result will be (verses 5-6)?

3. In this psalm there are five other things David asks of God (verses 7-12). What are they?

Interpretation

4. What does David start this psalm by focusing on? Why do you think he begins this way?

5. What do you think it means to dwell in the house of the Lord (verse 4)? Does it mean staying at church all the time? Or what?

6. What in this psalm does David say he does to face his fear? What is his strategy?

leader!

7. Does David get his answer by the end of the psalm? What does this tell you about the way the Lord works?

Application

8. When in your life have you been the most afraid? What did you do to handle it?

9. Have you ever had the experience of sensing God's presence when you were afraid? What was it like?

10. Why do you think we have to wait for the Lord (verse 14)? What happens to us when we wait? What reasons could God possibly have for making us wait?

HELP! i'm a s

THE PARABLE OF THE SOWER
MARK 4

Observation

1. Who did Jesus tell this parable to? Where was he when he told it (verse 1)?

2. This parable is about a farmer, some seed, and several types of soil. Of these three "players," which two remain constant throughout the story? Which one changes? How does it change?

3. Why does Jesus say he speaks in parables (verse 12)? How does that relate to what he says in verse 9?

Interpretation

4. Who do you think the farmer is in this parable? What does the seed represent?

5. What kinds of people are represented by the four soils? Do you know any people like this?

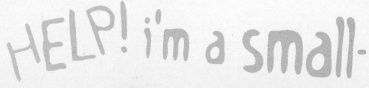

122

6. Why do you think Jesus told this story? How do you think people felt when they heard it?

7. What did Jesus mean when he said, "He who has ears to hear, let him hear"?

Application

8. Which soil best represents you at this time?

   ❑ The path—you don't really feel a need for God or his Word

   ❑ Rocky soil—you've made a commitment, but your faith is pretty shallow

   ❑ Soil with thorns—you've made a commitment, but other things are crowding it out and distracting you

   ❑ Deep soil—you've made a commitment and are truly living out your faith

9. Which soil best represents where you'd like to be?

10. What would it take for you to get there? (changing priorities, getting some new friends, support from your family, etc.)

group leader!

EPHESIANS
CHAPTER 1

Observation

1. According to verses 3-9, what things has God given us?

2. Verse 4 says we were chosen by God. According to this verse, *when* did this happen? What does this verse say about *why* we were chosen?

3. Look at verses 11-12. What do these verses say about why we were chosen? What was God's purpose in choosing us?

Interpretation

4. Do you think it's actually possible for us to be holy and blameless in God's sight (verse 4)? Why or why not? How does verse 7 tie in with this?

5. What do you think it means to be chosen by God (verses 4-5, 11-12)? What effect does this have on our lives, if any?

6. According to verses 5-6, why did God want us to be his children? What does this tell you about the way God feels about us?

Application

7. When you become a Christian, what plan does your life become a part of (verses 11-12)? How do you see yourself fitting in to God's purpose for the world?

8. What goals do you have for your life? Does being a Christian affect the goals you have for your life? Why or why not?

9. Do you feel you play a significant role in life today? Why or why not?

10. What are some things you could do to make your life more significant? (Be specific!) What would it take for you to do these things?

FRIENDSHIP

Opening discussion

1. Think of a friendship, present or past, that has been important to you. What was it that made that friendship special?

2. What would you say are the three most important qualities of good friendship? Why are they important?

Observation/Interpretation

Read 1 Samuel chapter 20, then answer these questions:

3. How did David and Jonathan show their commitment to each other?

4. Who do you think was in the hardest position? Why?

5. Think about the feelings that Jonathan had toward David, who was clearly to be the next king—instead of Jonathan, the king's son. Have you ever had a friendship where your friend got something *you* wanted? How did you handle it?

6. What are some things you could do to stay committed to a friendship if you were in Jonathan's predicament? Or if you were in David's predicament?

7. Verse 17 says that Jonathan loved David as he loved himself. What do you think this means? Have you ever loved a friend that way?

Application

8. Read Proverbs 11:13 and James 4:11. What do these verses warn us about? Do you struggle with this in your friendships? What kind of friend are you?

9. Read Matthew 5:23-24. Is there anyone you need to go to in order to make things right with them? If so, are you ready to do it? What will you do?

10. Read Ecclesiastes 4:9-10. Do you have the kind of friend described in these verses? Are you the kind of friend that is described in these verses? Do you need to work more at being a better friend or getting better friends—or both?

HELP! i'm a small-group leader!

FAMILY

Opening discussion

1. Which of these four words best describes communication in your home: *nonexistent, argumentative, superficial, open.* Explain your answer.

2. What frustrates you the most about your parents? What do you appreciate most about him or her?

3. If you could change one thing about your home life, what would it be? Why?

Observation/interpretation

4. Read Ephesians 6:1-3. Do you have trouble with these verses? Why or why not?

5. Verse 3 explains the result of verses 1-2. Have you experienced this to be true? Why or why not?

6. In Ephesians 6:1 Paul says to obey your parents *in the Lord.* What does this mean? Is there ever a time when you shouldn't obey your parents? What about if they tell you to do something destructive or abusive?

7. Read Exodus 20:12. What does it mean to honor your father and mother? Can you disagree with your parents and still honor him or her? How?

8. Read Proverbs 19:20. What does this verse suggest about how we should respond to our parents? When is this particularly difficult to do?

Application

9. Romans 12:9-18 lists some Christian behaviors that we are to put into practice. Which of the following behaviors are the hardest for you to live out in your home?

   ❏ Unselfishness (versus doing your own thing)

   ❏ A good attitude (versus talking back, complaining, etc.)

   ❏ Patience (versus frustration or anger)

   ❏ Unconditional love (versus only loving when they give you what you want)

10. What are some things you could do this week to begin living out your faith more at home?

HELP! i'm

SELF-IMAGE

Opening discussion

1. If someone says, "Tell me about yourself," what are the first three things you'd say?

2. Do you think someone would have a good idea of who you are based on what you just said? Why or why not?

3. What affects the way you feel about yourself the most—your parents, friends, school, or the media (TV, magazines, movies)? Why?

Observation/interpretation

4. Read Psalm 139:13-16. What does this passage say about the way God created you? Do you feel the same way David does in verse 14? Why or why not?

5. How does this psalm affect the way you feel about yourself? Are you grateful to God, or angry with him? Explain.

6. Read 1 Samuel 16:7. How does God's view of us compare to the way we view each other? Whose view has a bigger impact on the way you feel?

7. The following three stories deal with people in Scripture whose actions showed that they struggled with their self-esteem. Read at least one of these stories: Zaccheus (Luke 19:1-10); the woman at the well (John 4:1-26); the woman caught in adultery (John 8:1-11). Now answer these questions about the story (or stories) you read:

    o What evidence do you find that this person struggled with their self-image?

    o How did Jesus attempt to heal their woundedness? What did he say? What did he do?

    o Do you relate to this person at all? If so, how?

Application

8. Does the way you feel about yourself affect the way you treat others? If so, how?

9. Why do you think it's important for us to have a healthy self-image? Do you have one? What, if anything, would make it better?

10. If God were to talk to you about the way you feel about yourself, what would he say? What would you say back to him?

a small-gr

LOVE, SEX & DATING

Opening discussion

1. What do you think it means to be in love? Is there a difference between *loving* someone and being *in love* with someone? If so, what?

2. Do you think sex between unmarried people is more an expression of love or of desire? Is there a difference?

3. When teenagers have sex, do you think they are doing it more for the other person or for themselves?

Observation/interpretation

4. Look up 1 Corinthians 13:4-7. What words are used to describe love? Is this definition compatible with the love you see most often in high school (or junior high) relationships? If not, how is it different?

5. Read Genesis 1:26-28. Based on this passage, what would you say is God's attitude toward sex? Do you think he thinks it's good or bad? When is it good? When is it bad?

6. Read Genesis 2:19-24. Verse 24 says that when a man and his wife come together, they become one flesh. Do you think two people who have sex with each other become one flesh even if they're not married to each other? Why or why not?

7. Read 1 Thessalonians 4:3-7. What do you think is meant here by sexual immorality? Why do you think so many people indulge in sexual immorality? Do you think it makes people feel more fulfilled or less fulfilled? Why?

8. Read 1 Corinthians 10:23-24. How might these verses help us with our sexual desires? According to verse 24, what should guide our behavior?

Application

9. Do you feel you are living out God's plan for your sexuality? If not, what do you need to do?

10. Which of your relationships have caused you to feel closer to God? Which have caused you to feel farther from him? Do any of your relationships need to change? What, if anything, are you going to do to begin making that change?

HELP! i'm a small-group

SHARING YOUR FAITH

Opening discussion

1. Have you ever had any experiences of sharing your faith? If so, how did it go? If not, why not?

2. When did you first hear about Christ? Who was it that told you? How did you respond?

3. If someone were to ask you how to become a Christian, what would you say?

Observation/Interpretation

4. Read Matthew 28:19-20. What in these verses does Jesus tell *us* to do? What does *he* promise to do?

5. In Matthew 4:19 Jesus explained to his disciples that they would become fishers not of fish, but of people. What do you think he meant by that?

6. Read Matthew 5:13. What does it mean to be salt? What does this have to do with sharing your faith? What does it mean for Christians to lose their saltiness? (Give specific examples.)

7. Read Matthew 5:14. How do Christians resemble light? Do you know any Christians that shine brightly? Describe one.

Application

8. When it comes to sharing your faith, do you feel more like a searchlight, a spotlight, or a flashlight? Why?

9. Using John 3:16, try to explain in your own words what it means to be a Christian. (Use additional Bible verses if you want.)

10. Think of a person you'd like to share your faith with. What is one step you could take toward making that happen?

RESOURCES FROM YOUTH SPECIALTIES

Professional Resources
Administration, Publicity, & Fundraising (Ideas Library)
Developing Student Leaders
Equipped to Serve: Volunteer Youth Worker Training Course
Help! I'm a Junior High Youth Worker!
Help! I'm a Small-Group Leader!
Help! I'm a Sunday School Teacher!
Help! I'm a Volunteer Youth Worker!
How to Expand Your Youth Ministry
How to Speak to Youth...and Keep Them Awake at the Same Time
Junior High Ministry (Updated & Expanded)
One Kid at a Time: Reaching Youth through Mentoring
Purpose-Driven Youth Ministry
So That's Why I Keep Doing This! 52 Devotional Stories for Youth Workers
A Youth Ministry Crash Course
The Youth Worker's Handbook to Family Ministry

Youth Ministry Programming
Camps, Retreats, Missions, & Service Ideas (Ideas Library)
Compassionate Kids: Practical Ways to Involve Your Students in Mission and Service
Creative Bible Lessons from the Old Testament
Creative Bible Lessons in John: Encounters with Jesus
Creative Bible Lessons in Romans: Faith on Fire!
Creative Bible Lessons on the Life of Christ
Creative Junior High Programs from A to Z, Vol. 1 (A-M)
Creative Junior High Programs from A to Z, Vol. 2 (N-Z)
Creative Meetings, Bible Lessons, & Worship Ideas (Ideas Library)
Crowd Breakers & Mixers (Ideas Library)
Drama, Skits, & Sketches (Ideas Library)
Dramatic Pauses
Facing Your Future: Graduating Youth Group with a Faith That Lasts
Games (Ideas Library)
Games 2 (Ideas Library)
Great Fundraising Ideas for Youth Groups
More Great Fundraising Ideas for Youth Groups
Great Retreats for Youth Groups
Greatest Skits on Earth
Greatest Skits on Earth, Vol. 2
Holiday Ideas (Ideas Library)
Hot Illustrations for Youth Talks
More Hot Illustrations for Youth Talks
Incredible Questionnaires for Youth Ministry
Junior High Game Nights
More Junior High Game Nights
Kickstarters: 101 Ingenious Intros to Just about Any Bible Lesson
Live the Life! Student Evangelism Training Kit

continued on next page

Memory Makers
Play It! Great Games for Groups
Play It Again! More Great Games for Groups
Special Events (Ideas Library)
Spontaneous Melodramas
Super Sketches for Youth Ministry
Teaching the Bible Creatively
What Would Jesus Do? Youth Leader's Kit
Wild Truth Bible Lessons
Wild Truth Bible Lessons 2
Worship Services for Youth Groups

Discussion Starters
Discussion & Lesson Starters (Ideas Library)
Discussion & Lesson Starters 2 (Ideas Library)
Get 'Em Talking
Keep 'Em Talking!
High School TalkSheets
More High School TalkSheets
High School TalkSheets: Psalms and Proverbs
Junior High TalkSheets
More Junior High TalkSheets
Junior High TalkSheets: Psalms and Proverbs
What If...? 450 Thought-Provoking Questions to Get Teenagers Talking, Laughing,
  and Thinking
Would You Rather...? 465 Provocative Questions to Get Teenagers Talking
Have You Ever...? 450 Intriguing Questions Guaranteed to Get Teenagers Talking

Clip Art
ArtSource Vol. 1—Fantastic Activities
ArtSource Vol. 2—Borders, Symbols, Holidays, and Attention Getters
ArtSource Vol. 3—Sports
ArtSource Vol. 4—Phrases and Verses
ArtSource Vol. 5—Amazing Oddities and Appalling Images
ArtSource Vol. 6—Spiritual Topics
ArtSource Vol. 7—Variety Pack
ArtSource Vol. 8—Stark Raving Clip Art
ArtSource Vols. 1-7 on CD-ROM
ArtSource Vol. 8 & Promo Kit on CD-ROM

Videos
EdgeTV
The Heart of Youth Ministry: A Morning with Mike Yaconelli
Next Time I Fall in Love Video Curriculum
Understanding Your Teenager Video Curriculum

Student Books
Grow For It Journal
Grow For It Journal through the Scriptures
What Would Jesus Do? Spiritual Challenge Journal
Wild Truth Journal for Junior Highers